THE COMPUTER GRAPHICS BOOK
FOR SENIORS AND BEGINNERS

by

Prof. Alfonso J. Kinglow

ISBN - 13: 978-1539749417
ISBN – 10: 153974-941X

Printed in the United States of America

DEDICATION

This book is dedicated to all the Seniors
and beginners who encouraged me to put all my
Computer Graphics in one place for
easy understanding of Computer Technology
and to expand my vision.

PREFACE

I began to develop a format for my books called .gbf or Graphics Box Format, where I use Graphics to teach and explain Computer Technology to beginners and users with some knowledge of Computers.

Graphics Box Format could be the next Standard in Desktop Publishing, most of all my Graphics were design with No.2 pencil and scanned as .PDF documents.

The goal is for the student to look at the Graphic page and be able to identify the main components while putting them all together to convey a better understanding of the Technology, Students will then not necessarily have to read 3 of 5 pages of Text to understand what is going on and how the system works.

My Graphics are scanned at 300 to 600 dpi in high resolution, for easy reading. Information is broken down into graphics boxes with input and output links. These graphic boxes are active objects on the graphic pages, with clear text and are integrated into an algorithm to connect the graphics with holographic Software been developed, of which some are now available at the publication date of this book.

The Hololens and Holographic scanner is been developed by Microsoft and will be available later on this year.
Graphic Box Format (.gbf) is been reviewed, and later will be able to Convert Graphics back to Text, in its original form.

For now it is my hope that the Graphics will clarify, expand and explain in a very simple and visual way how technology works, and facilitate the clear understanding of Computers for students as well as for advanced users.

Graphics is a visual tool used by Teachers and all Educators to convey information rapidly and makes it easy to understand Concepts in Computer Technology.

My goal is to develop the graphics for it to be interactive and holographic so that it can be manipulated to expand the understanding of how text and graphic interact and can be connected to manipulate data, above the page.

Using my Convert program and algorithm, graphics in .gbf will be able to be converted back to text, and retain its original formatting.

Graphics Box Format is mentioned in my books " Not Just Another Computer Book Two" and also in "Not Just Another Computer Book For Advanced Users".

More information will be available later about this new technology in my next book.

ONE
Concept

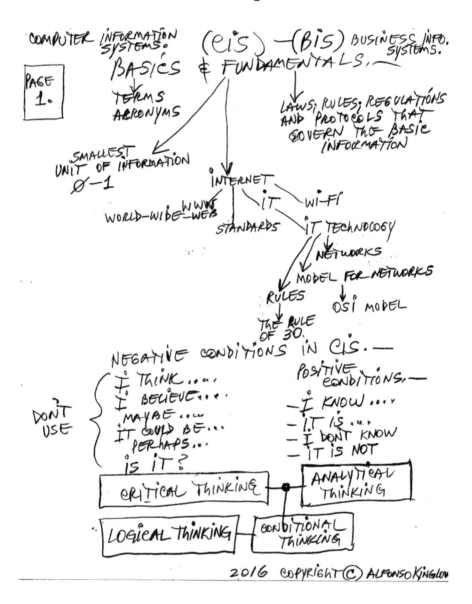

COMPUTER INFORMATION SYSTEMS. (eis) — (bis) BUSINESS INFO. SYSTEMS.

BASICS & FUNDAMENTALS. —

PAGE 1.

TERMS
ACRONYMS

LAWS; RULES; REGULATIONS
AND PROTOCOLS THAT
GOVERN THE BASIC
INFORMATION

SMALLEST
UNIT OF INFORMATION
∅ — 1

INTERNET

WORLD—WIDE—WEB   WWW

IT   WI-FI

STANDARDS   IT TECHNOLOGY

NETWORKS

MODEL FOR NETWORKS

RULES

OSI MODEL

THE RULE
OF 30.

NEGATIVE CONDITIONS IN CIS. —

DON'T
USE

I THINK....
I BELIEVE....
MAYBE....
IT COULD BE...
PERHAPS...
IS IT?

POSITIVE
CONDITIONS. —

— I KNOW ....
— IT IS ....
— I DON'T KNOW
— IT IS NOT

CRITICAL THINKING   ANALYTICAL THINKING

LOGICAL THINKING   CONDITIONAL THINKING

TWO
Actual

WHAT CAN COMPUTERS DO. —

PAGE 2.

BASIC COMPUTERS CAN NOT, AND ARE NOT:
- DUMB TERMINALS
- GAME MACHINES
- JUST HARDWARE
- JUST SOFTWARE
- CAN NOT DIVIDE BY ZERO (0).
- NECESSARY MACHINES TO SOME PEOPLE.
- EMPTY BOXES WITH INPUT AND OUTPUT
- IMUNE TO SICKNESS OR INFECTIONS VIRUSES
- WILL NOT LAST FOREVER.
- SECURE ALL THE TIME.

CAN AND COMPUTERS ARE:
- TASK DRIVEN MACHINES
- ANALYTICAL
- ARE INTELLIGENT
- USE THEIR OWN LANGUAGE. (BINARY)
- UNDERSTANDS ENGLISH
- UNIVERSAL MACHINES
- HAVE MEMORY
- REMEMBERS
- FIRST LINE OF DEFENSE
- PART OF THE "GRID"
- FAST, EFFICIENT WHEN USED CORRECTLY.
- USE MOM & DAD
- USE SPYS TO COMMUNICATE/REPORT
- CAN TALK, SPEAK
- THEY GIVE ACCESS, RIGHTS, PRIVILEGE, AND PERMISSIONS.
- HAVE A UNIVERSAL PASSWORD. AMEN
- HAVE A UNIVERSAL "TEST USER"/WORD HELLO
- WITH PROPER SOFTWARE. SECURE MACHINES
- HAVE LOCK AND KEY
- HELP US TO BE MORE PRODUCTIVE.

CONTINUE ——→

THREE
Actual Two

c's.

COMPUTERS... (CONTINUE)
ARE AND CAN...

- USE PROTOCOLS TO COMMUNICATE
- USE STANDARDS
- CAN LOCK YOU OUT
- TALK TO SATELLITES
- CAN FIND YOU
- KNOW'S WHERE YOU ARE..
- CAN SEE YOU
- CAN READ/WRITE TO YOU
- SEND/ YOUR MAIL AND
  RECEIVE MAIL
- CAN PLAY
- CAN BE SUPER-COMPUTERS
- ARE USED BY ALL AGES
- ARE MULTI-LINGUAL
- ARE TEACHING MACHINES
- HAVE A HEART, ITS CALLED C/U.
- THINK FASTER.
- GET SICK WITH VIRUSES
- CAN BE INOCULATED
- USER FRIENDLY

Introduction to Graphics
in GBF

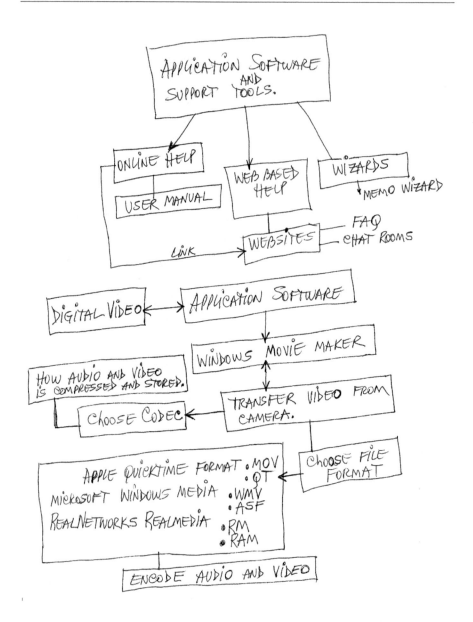

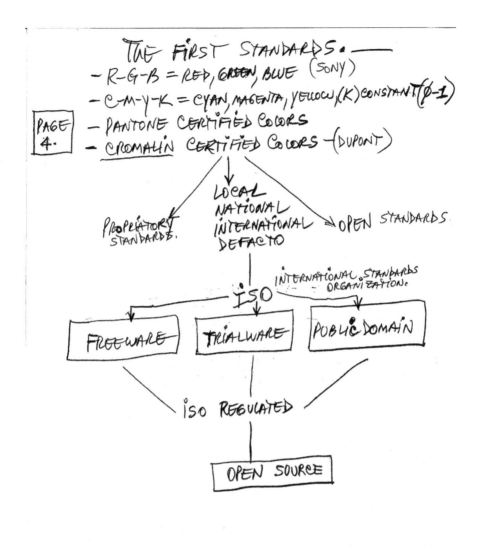

THE FIRST STANDARDS. —
- R-G-B = RED, GREEN, BLUE (SONY)
- C-M-Y-K = CYAN, MAGENTA, YELLOW, (K) CONSTANT ($0-1$)
- PANTONE CERTIFIED COLORS
- CROMALIN CERTIFIED COLORS — (DUPONT)

PAGE 4.

PROPRIATORY STANDARDS.

LOCAL
NATIONAL
INTERNATIONAL
DEFACTO

OPEN STANDARDS.

ISO
INTERNATIONAL STANDARDS ORGANIZATION.

FREEWARE   TRIALWARE   PUBLIC DOMAIN

ISO REGULATED

OPEN SOURCE

FIVE

COMPUTER VIRUSSES.—

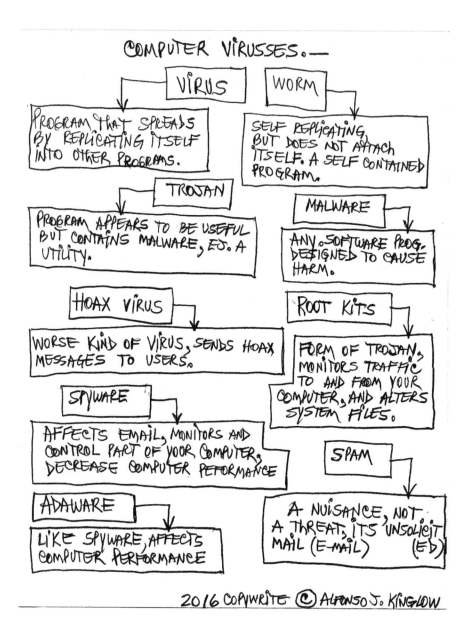

VIRUS — PROGRAM THAT SPREADS BY REPLICATING ITSELF INTO OTHER PROGRAMS.

WORM — SELF REPLICATING, BUT DOES NOT ATTACH ITSELF. A SELF CONTAINED PROGRAM.

TROJAN — PROGRAM APPEARS TO BE USEFUL BUT CONTAINS MALWARE, EJ. A UTILITY.

MALWARE — ANY. SOFTWARE PROG. DESIGNED TO CAUSE HARM.

HOAX VIRUS — WORSE KIND OF VIRUS, SENDS HOAX MESSAGES TO USERS.

ROOT KITS — FORM OF TROJAN, MONITORS TRAFFIC TO AND FROM YOUR COMPUTER, AND ALTERS SYSTEM FILES.

SPYWARE — AFFECTS EMAIL, MONITORS AND CONTROL PART OF YOUR COMPUTER, DECREASE COMPUTER PEFORMANCE

SPAM — A NUISANCE, NOT A THREAT, ITS UNSOLICIT MAIL (E-MAIL) (ED)

ADAWARE — LIKE SPYWARE, AFFECTS COMPUTER PERFORMANCE

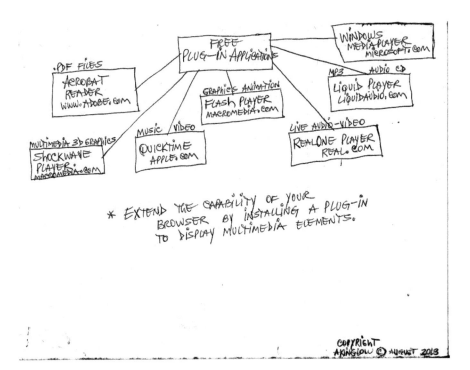

FREE
PLUG-IN APPLICATIONS

WINDOWS
MEDIA PLAYER
MICROSOFT.COM

.PDF FILES
ACROBAT
READER
WWW.ADOBE.COM

GRAPHICS ANIMATION
FLASH PLAYER
MACROMEDIA.COM

MP3   AUDIO CD
LIQUID PLAYER
LIQUIDAUDIO.COM

MULTIMEDIA 3D GRAPHICS
SHOCKWAVE
PLAYER
MACROMEDIA.COM

MUSIC   VIDEO
QUICKTIME
APPLE.COM

LIVE AUDIO-VIDEO
REALONE PLAYER
REAL.COM

* EXTEND THE CAPABILITY OF YOUR
BROWSER BY INSTALLING A PLUG-IN
TO DISPLAY MULTIMEDIA ELEMENTS.

SEVEN

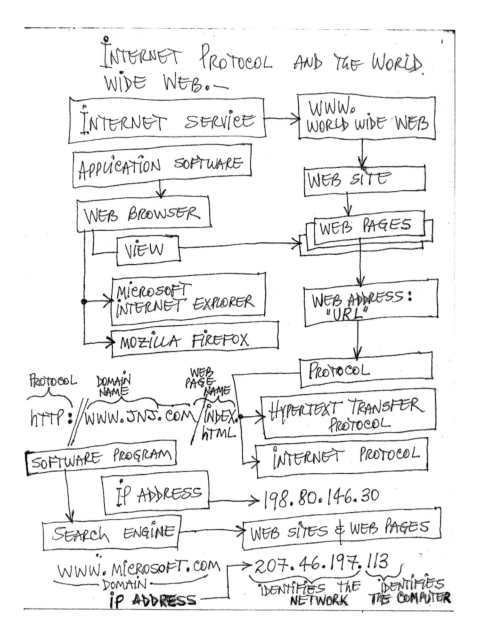

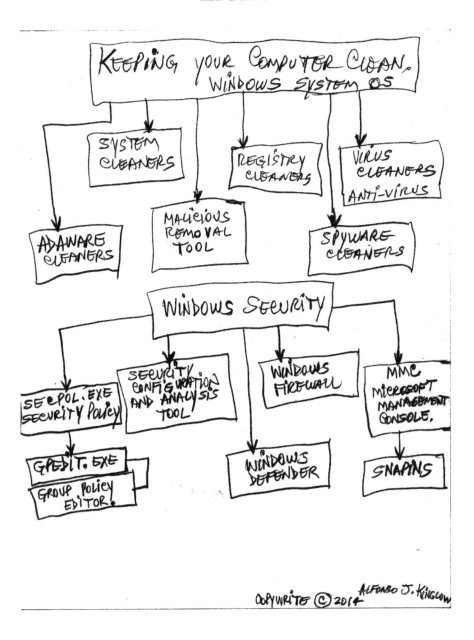

NINE

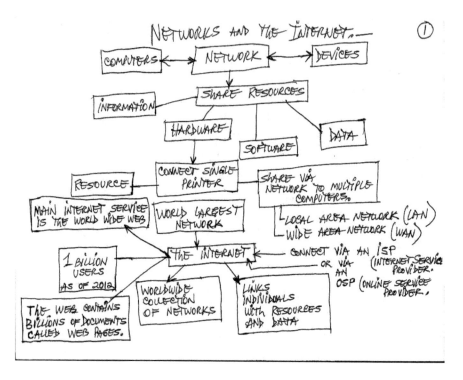

NETWORKS AND THE INTERNET. — ①

COMPUTERS ← NETWORK ← → DEVICES

SHARE RESOURCES

INFORMATION

HARDWARE

SOFTWARE

DATA

CONNECT SINGLE PRINTER

RESOURCE

SHARE VIA NETWORK TO MULTIPLE COMPUTERS.

MAIN INTERNET SERVICE IS THE WORLD WIDE WEB

WORLD LARGEST NETWORK

– LOCAL AREA NETWORK (LAN)
– WIDE AREA NETWORK (WAN)

1 BILLION USERS AS OF 2012

THE INTERNET

CONNECT VIA AN ISP
OR VIA (INTERNET SERVICE AN PROVIDER.
OSP (ONLINE SERVICE PROVIDER.

THE WEB CONTAINS BILLIONS OF DOCUMENTS CALLED WEB PAGES.

WORLDWIDE COLLECTION OF NETWORKS

LINKS INDIVIDUALS WITH RESOURCES AND DATA

TEN

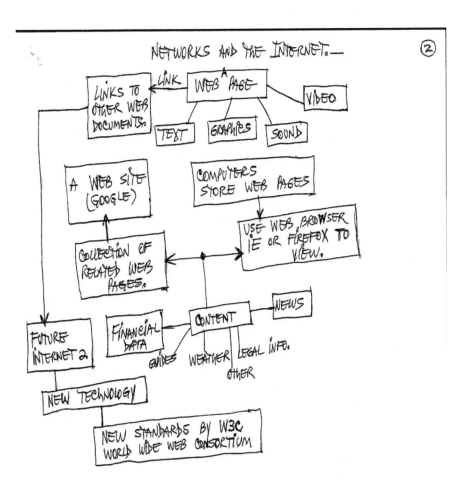

ELEVEN

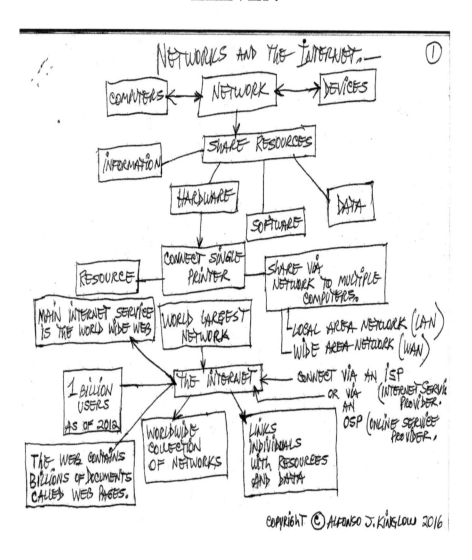

Networks and the Internet.— ①

COMPUTERS ← → NETWORK ← → DEVICES

INFORMATION — SHARE RESOURCES

HARDWARE — SOFTWARE — DATA

CONNECT SINGLE PRINTER

RESOURCE

SHARE VIA NETWORK TO MULTIPLE COMPUTERS.

└ LOCAL AREA NETWORK (LAN)
└ WIDE AREA NETWORK (WAN)

MAIN INTERNET SERVICE IS THE WORLD WIDE WEB

WORLD LARGEST NETWORK

THE INTERNET ← CONNECT VIA AN ISP
OR VIA AN (INTERNET SERVICE PROVIDER.
OSP (ONLINE SERVICE PROVIDER.

1 BILLION USERS AS OF 2012

WORLDWIDE COLLECTION OF NETWORKS

LINKS INDIVIDUALS WITH RESOURCES AND DATA

THE WEB CONTAINS BILLIONS OF DOCUMENTS CALLED WEB PAGES.

COPYRIGHT © ALFONSO J. KINGLOW 2016

TWELVE

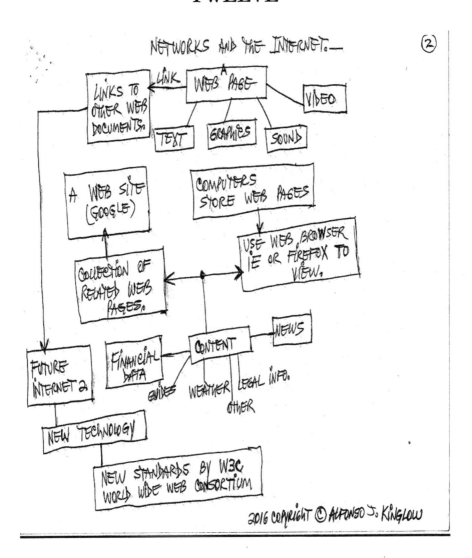

NETWORKS AND THE INTERNET.

(2)

LINK — WEB PAGE

LINKS TO OTHER WEB DOCUMENTS.

VIDEO

TEXT   GRAPHICS   SOUND

A WEB SITE (GOOGLE)

COMPUTERS STORE WEB PAGES

USE WEB BROWSER IE OR FIREFOX TO VIEW.

COLLECTION OF RELATED WEB PAGES.

FUTURE INTERNET 2

FINANCIAL DATA

CONTENT

NEWS

GUIDES   WEATHER   LEGAL INFO.

OTHER

NEW TECHNOLOGY

NEW STANDARDS BY W3C WORLD WIDE WEB CONSORTIUM

THIRTEEN

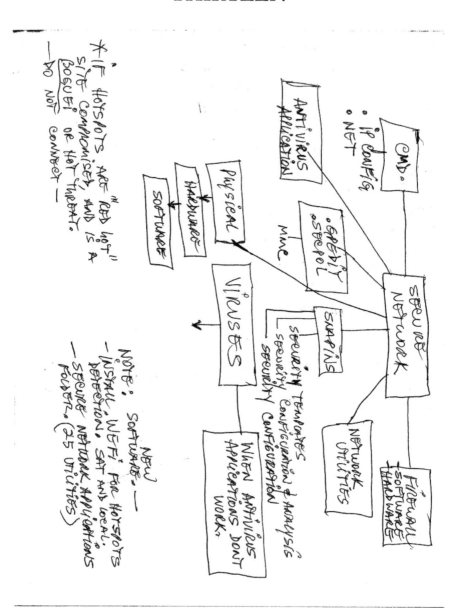

FOURTEEN

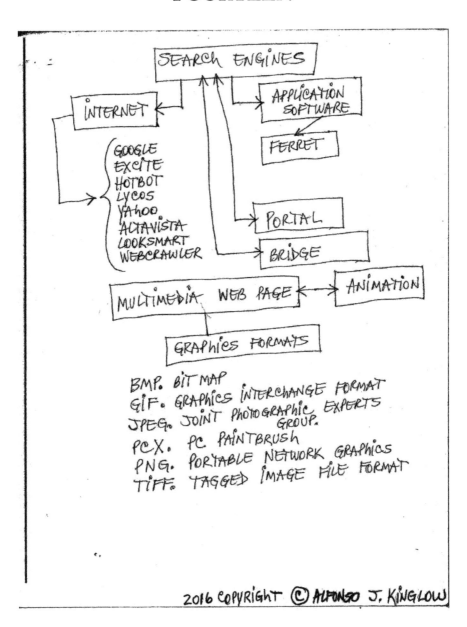

SEARCH ENGINES

INTERNET

APPLICATION SOFTWARE

FERRET

GOOGLE
EXCITE
HOTBOT
LYCOS
YAHOO
ALTAVISTA
LOOKSMART
WEBCRAWLER

PORTAL

BRIDGE

MULTIMEDIA WEB PAGE

ANIMATION

GRAPHICS FORMATS

BMP. BIT MAP
GIF. GRAPHICS INTERCHANGE FORMAT
JPEG. JOINT PHOTOGRAPHIC EXPERTS GROUP.
PCX. PC PAINTBRUSH
PNG. PORTABLE NETWORK GRAPHICS
TIFF. TAGGED IMAGE FILE FORMAT

FIFTEEN

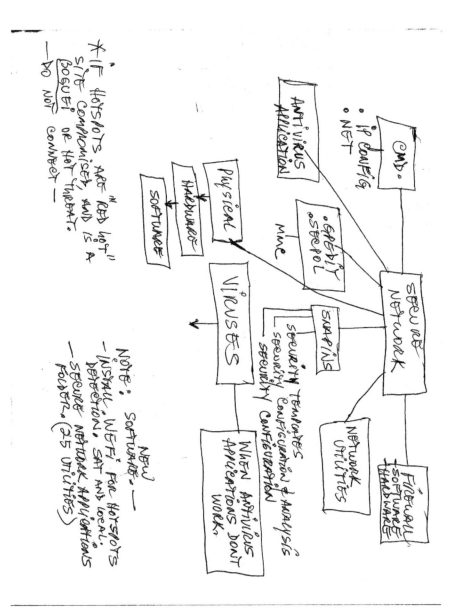

CMD.
· IP CONFIG
· NET

ANTIVIRUS APPLICATION

* IF HOTSPOTS ARE "RED HOT"
SITE COMPROMISED, AND IS A
ROGUE OR HOT THREAT.
— DO NOT CONNECT —

PHYSICAL

HARDWARE

SOFTWARE

SPECIFY
· SECPOL
MMC

VIRUSES

SNAPINS

SECURE
NETWORK

SECURITY TEMPLATES
SECURITY CONFIGURATION & ANALYSIS
SECURITY CONFIGURATION

NETWORK
UTILITIES

FIREWALL
SOFTWARE
HARDWARE

WHEN ANTIVIRUS
APPLICATIONS DON'T
WORK.

NEW
NOTE: SOFTWARE —
— INSTALL WIFI FOR HOTSPOTS
PROTECTION, SAT AND LOCAL.
— SECURE NETWORK APPLICATIONS
FOLDER. (25 UTILITIES)

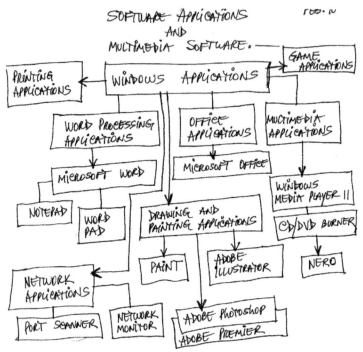

SOFTWARE APPLICATIONS AND MULTIMEDIA SOFTWARE. — FIG. IV

NOTE:
INSTALL APPLICATIONS vs. RUN APPLICATIONS
UNINSTALL APPLICATIONS vs. DELETE APPLICATIONS
ADD AND REMOVE APPLICATIONS (SOFTWARE)
UTILITY vs. APPLICATIONS
USER INSTALL vs. SYSTEM INSTALL APPLICATIONS

SEVENTEEN

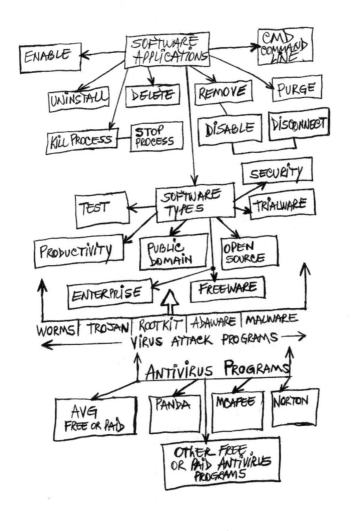

EIGHTEEN

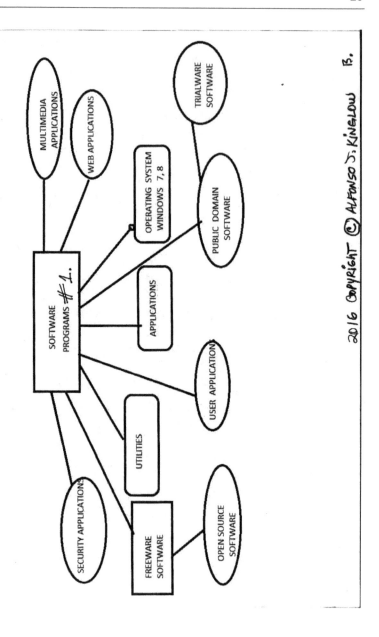

NINETEEN

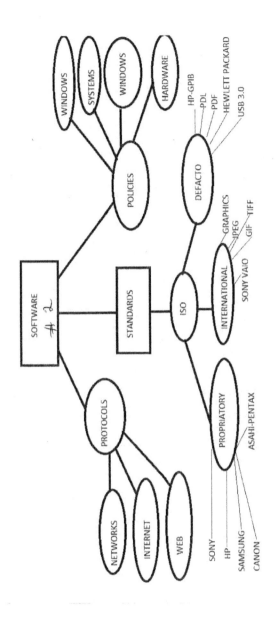

TWENTY

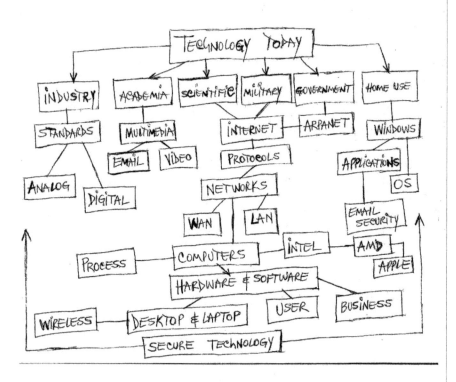

TWENTY ONE

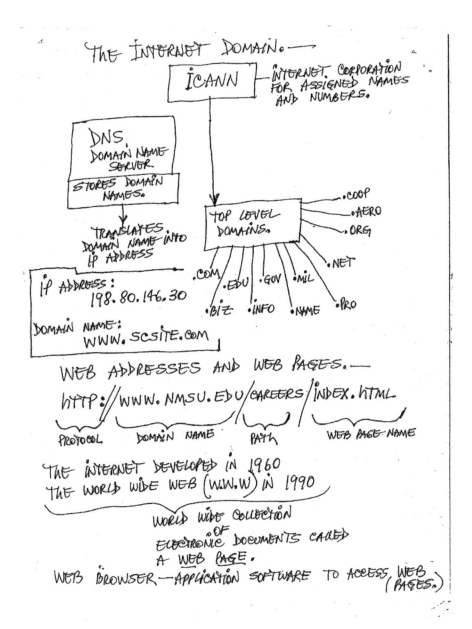

THE INTERNET DOMAIN. —

ICANN — INTERNET CORPORATION FOR ASSIGNED NAMES AND NUMBERS.

DNS. DOMAIN NAME SERVER
STORES DOMAIN NAMES.

TRANSLATES DOMAIN NAME INTO IP ADDRESS

TOP LEVEL DOMAINS.

.COOP
.AERO
.ORG
.NET
.COM
.EDU
.GOV
.MIL
.PRO
.BIZ
.INFO
.NAME

IP ADDRESS: 198.80.146.30
DOMAIN NAME: WWW.SCSITE.COM

WEB ADDRESSES AND WEB PAGES. —

hTTP://WWW.NMSU.EDU/CAREERS/INDEX.HTML

PROTOCOL   DOMAIN NAME   PATH   WEB PAGE NAME

THE INTERNET DEVELOPED IN 1960
THE WORLD WIDE WEB (W.W.W) IN 1990

WORLD WIDE COLLECTION OF ELECTRONIC DOCUMENTS CALLED A WEB PAGE.

WEB BROWSER — APPLICATION SOFTWARE TO ACCESS WEB (PAGES.)

TWENTY TWO

ANALOG vs. DIGITAL.—

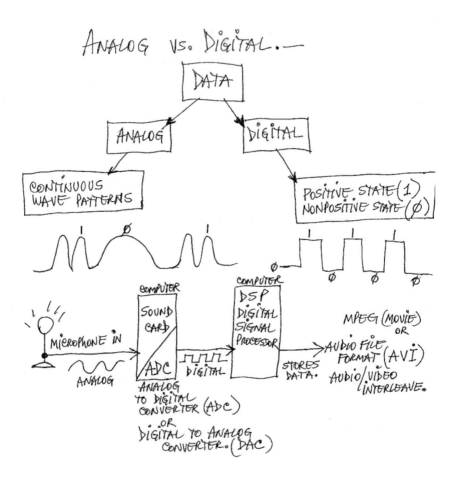

DATA

ANALOG

DIGITAL

CONTINUOUS WAVE PATTERNS

POSITIVE STATE (1)
NONPOSITIVE STATE (∅)

MICROPHONE IN

ANALOG

COMPUTER
SOUND CARD
ADC
DIGITAL

ANALOG TO DIGITAL CONVERTER (ADC)
.OR
DIGITAL TO ANALOG CONVERTER. (DAC)

COMPUTER
DSP
DIGITAL SIGNAL PROCESSOR

STORES DATA.

MPEG (MOVIE)
OR
AUDIO FILE FORMAT (AVI)
AUDIO/VIDEO INTERLEAVE.

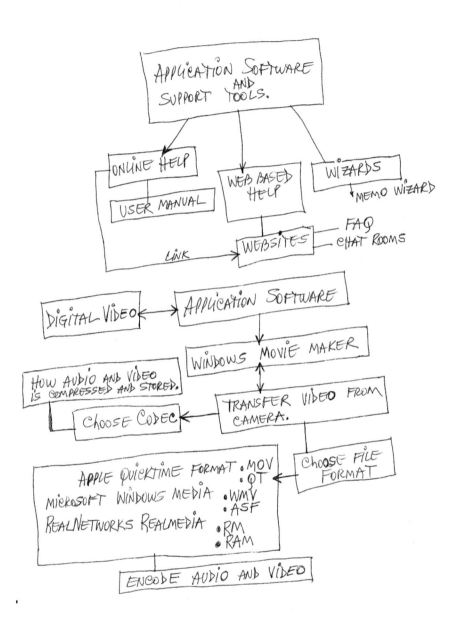

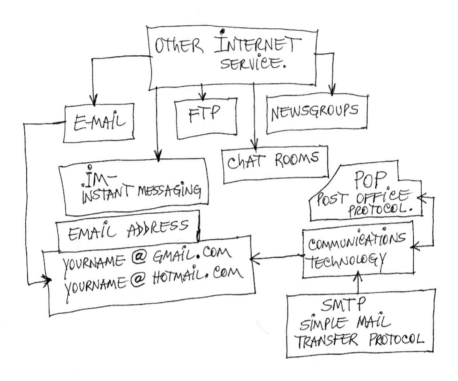

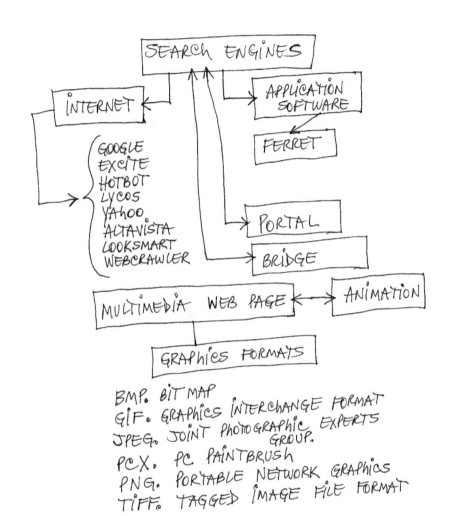

BMP. BIT MAP
GIF. GRAPHICS INTERCHANGE FORMAT
JPEG. JOINT PHOTOGRAPHIC EXPERTS
              GROUP.
PCX. PC PAINTBRUSH
PNG. PORTABLE NETWORK GRAPHICS
TIFF. TAGGED IMAGE FILE FORMAT

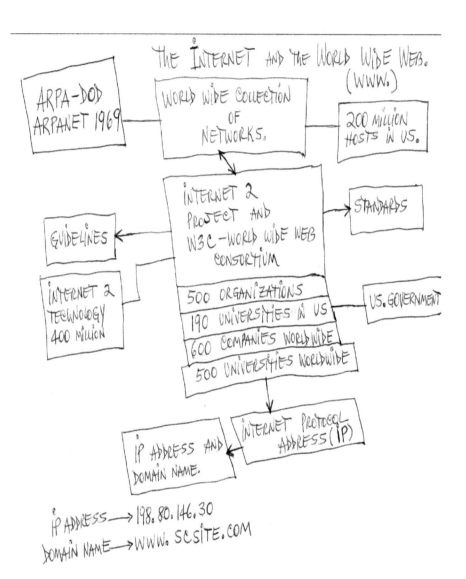

THE INTERNET AND THE WORLD WIDE WEB. (WWW.)

ARPA-DOD ARPANET 1969

WORLD WIDE COLLECTION OF NETWORKS.

200 MILLION HOSTS IN US.

INTERNET 2 PROJECT AND W3C - WORLD WIDE WEB CONSORTIUM

STANDARDS

GUIDELINES

INTERNET 2 TECHNOLOGY 400 MILLION

500 ORGANIZATIONS
190 UNIVERSITIES IN US
600 COMPANIES WORLDWIDE
500 UNIVERSITIES WORLDWIDE

US. GOVERNMENT

INTERNET PROTOCOL ADDRESS (IP)

IP ADDRESS AND DOMAIN NAME.

IP ADDRESS ⟶ 198. 80. 146. 30
DOMAIN NAME ⟶ WWW. SCSITE. COM

TWENTYSEVEN

Creating the All Applications Special Folder.

To create the all applications folder using the hidden embedded code in windows, create a blank folder and give it the name Applications, **put a period after the s.** and enter the following Code below.

**Start by using the "open bracket" {
enter the Code, and close the bracket }
and press <Enter>**

Applications.{4234d49b-0245-4df3-b780-3893943456e1}

enter.

The all applications folder will be created, this folder in windows will contain a lot of hidden graphics and graphics tools, you can use.

TWENTYEIGHT

The Secret Advanced Folder. __

To create the Secret Advanced folder hidden in Windows, create a blank folder and call it Advanced. Put a period after the d. Open bracket {

Enter the Code, then close bracket }

Enter the following Code:

Advanced. { ED7BA470-8E54-465E-825C-99712043E01C}

\<ENTER\>

The Advanced folder will be created, which contains over 250 files to fix and troubleshoot windows.

TWENTYNINE

Content of Advanced Folder after its creation.

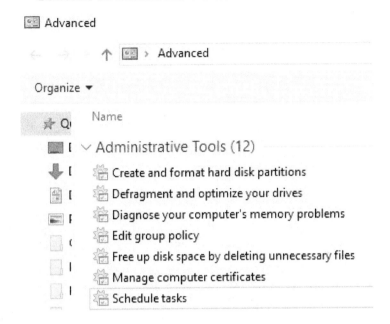

 Advanced

↑ > Advanced

Organize ▼

Name

⌄ Administrative Tools (12)

- Create and format hard disk partitions
- Defragment and optimize your drives
- Diagnose your computer's memory problems
- Edit group policy
- Free up disk space by deleting unnecessary files
- Manage computer certificates
- Schedule tasks

- Set up iSCSI initiator
- Set up ODBC data sources (32-bit)
- Set up ODBC data sources (64-bit)
- View event logs
- View local services

⌄ AutoPlay (3)

- Change default settings for media or devices
- Play CDs or other media automatically
- Start or stop using AutoPlay for all media and devices

⌄ Backup and Restore (Windows 7) (2)

- Backup and Restore (Windows 7)
- Restore data, files, or computer from backup (Windows 7)

⌄ BitLocker Drive Encryption (1)

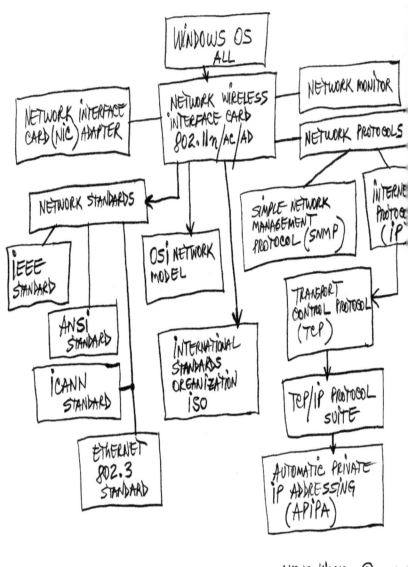

WINDOWS OS
ALL

NETWORK WIRELESS
INTERFACE CARD
802.11n/ac/AD

NETWORK INTERFACE
CARD (NIC) ADAPTER

NETWORK MONITOR

NETWORK PROTOCOLS

NETWORK STANDARDS

SIMPLE NETWORK
MANAGEMENT
PROTOCOL (SNMP)

INTERNE
PROTOC
(IP

IEEE
STANDARD

OSI NETWORK
MODEL

TRANSPORT
CONTROL PROTOCOL
(TCP)

ANSI
STANDARD

ICANN
STANDARD

INTERNATIONAL
STANDARDS
ORGANIZATION
ISO

TCP/IP PROTOCOL
SUITE

ETHERNET
802.3
STANDARD

AUTOMATIC PRIVATE
IP ADDRESSING
(APIPA)

BLANK PAGE

THIRTY

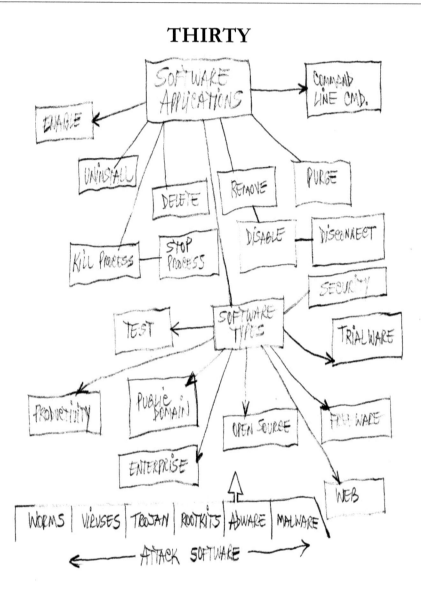

ALFONSO KINGMAN © 2015

THIRTYONE

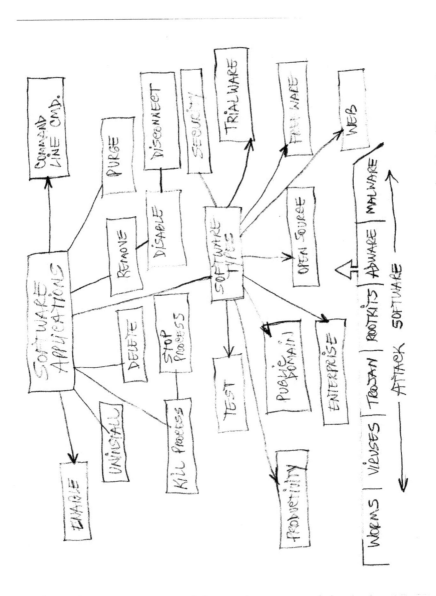

ALFONSO KINGSLEY © 2015

THIRTYTWO

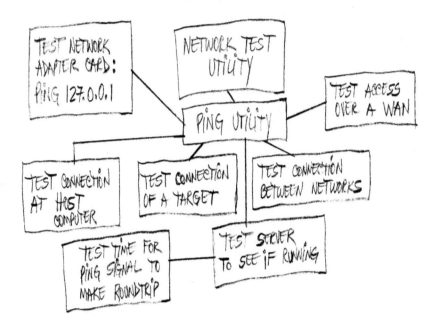

THIRTYTHREE

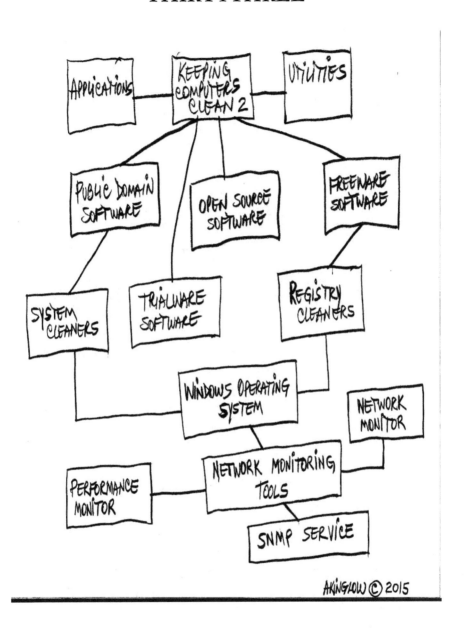

THIRTYFOUR

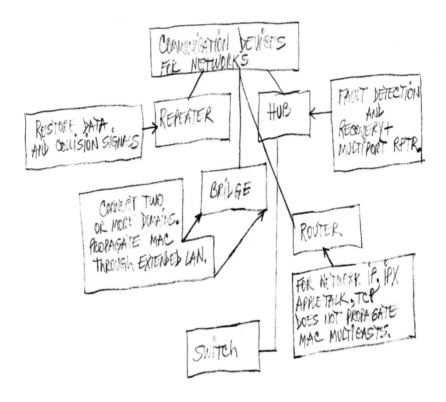

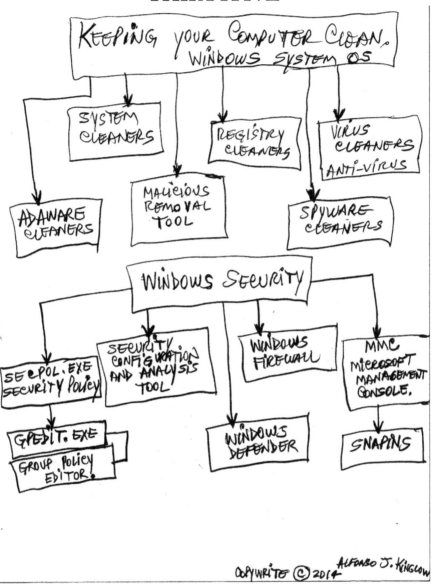

THIRTYSIX

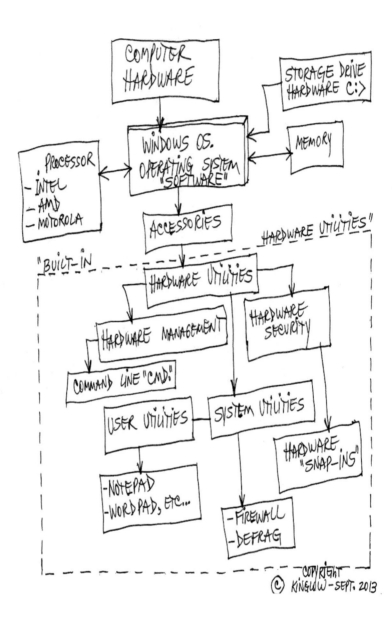

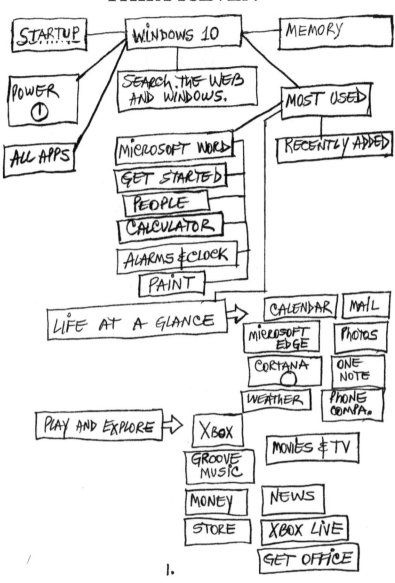

STARTUP — WINDOWS 10 — MEMORY

POWER ①

SEARCH. THE WEB AND WINDOWS.

MOST USED

ALL APPS

RECENTLY ADDED

MICROSOFT WORD
GET STARTED
PEOPLE
CALCULATOR
ALARMS & CLOCK
PAINT

LIFE AT A GLANCE →

CALENDAR | MAIL
MICROSOFT EDGE | PHOTOS
CORTANA | ONE NOTE
WEATHER | PHONE COMPA.

PLAY AND EXPLORE →

XBOX
GROOVE MUSIC
MONEY
STORE

MOVIES & TV

NEWS
XBOX LIVE
GET OFFICE

1.

THIRTYEIGHT

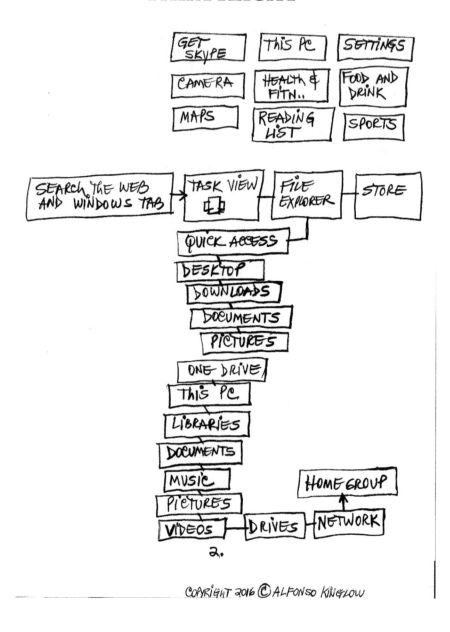

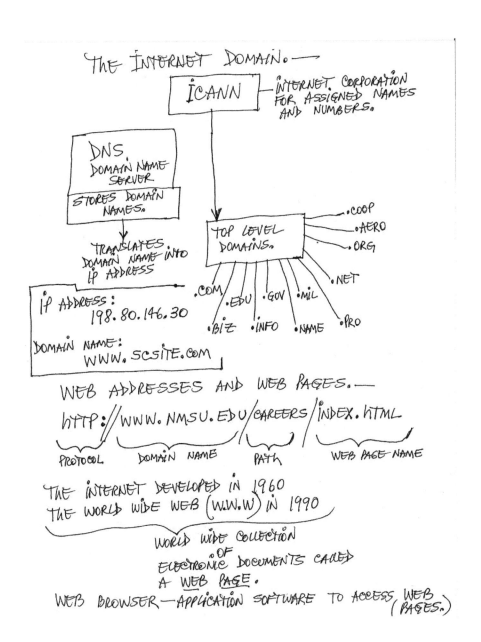

THE INTERNET DOMAIN.→

ICANN — INTERNET. CORPORATION FOR ASSIGNED NAMES AND NUMBERS.

DNS. DOMAIN NAME SERVER
STORES DOMAIN NAMES.

TRANSLATES DOMAIN NAME INTO IP ADDRESS

TOP LEVEL DOMAINS.
.COOP
.AERO
.ORG
.NET
.COM
.EDU
.GOV
.MIL
.BIZ
.INFO
.NAME
.PRO

IP ADDRESS: 198.80.146.30

DOMAIN NAME: WWW. SCSITE.COM

WEB ADDRESSES AND WEB PAGES.—

http://www.nmsu.edu/careers/index.html

PROTOCOL — DOMAIN NAME — PATH — WEB PAGE NAME

THE INTERNET DEVELOPED IN 1960
THE WORLD WIDE WEB (W.W.W) IN 1990

WORLD WIDE COLLECTION OF ELECTRONIC DOCUMENTS CALLED A WEB PAGE.

WEB BROWSER—APPLICATION SOFTWARE TO ACCESS WEB PAGES.

FORTY

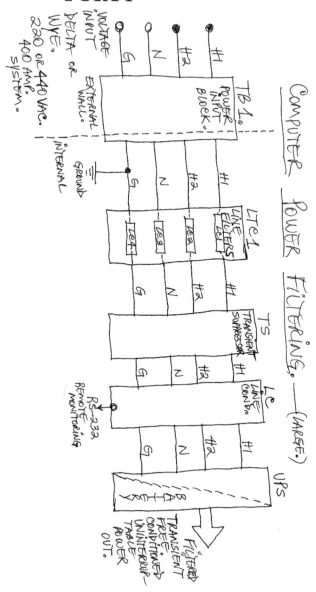

COMPUTER POWER FILTERING. — (LARGE.)

I have created forty-five different Graphic pages that represent various aspect of Computer Hardware and Software and also troubleshooting Graphics to aid in fixing computers that have problems.
The Advanced Graphic folder that the user can create in Windows contain all the information a user would ever need to troubleshoot and fix their own computer.

The main thing is understanding how computer works and why, also what to do when the Computer freezes and where to go. This makes the book completely different from the "How to" and from Manuals and user's Guide.

The intent of this book was never to make it a User's Guide or Manual, since such books do not teach anything useful to the user, beside there are many such books available in the marketplace.

FORTYONE

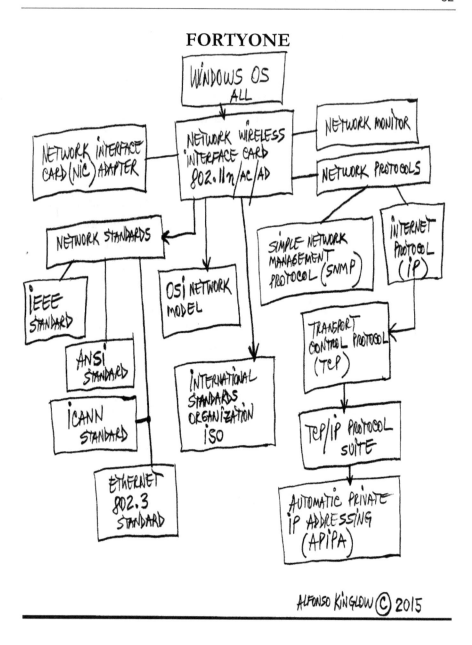

WINDOWS OS
ALL

NETWORK WIRELESS
INTERFACE CARD
802.11n/ac/AD

NETWORK INTERFACE
CARD (NIC) ADAPTER

NETWORK MONITOR

NETWORK PROTOCOLS

NETWORK STANDARDS

IEEE STANDARD

ANSI STANDARD

ICANN STANDARD

ETHERNET 802.3 STANDARD

OSI NETWORK MODEL

INTERNATIONAL STANDARDS ORGANIZATION ISO

SIMPLE NETWORK MANAGEMENT PROTOCOL (SNMP)

INTERNET PROTOCOL (IP)

TRANSPORT CONTROL PROTOCOL (TCP)

TCP/IP PROTOCOL SUITE

AUTOMATIC PRIVATE IP ADDRESSING (APIPA)

ALFONSO KINGLOW © 2015

FORTYTWO

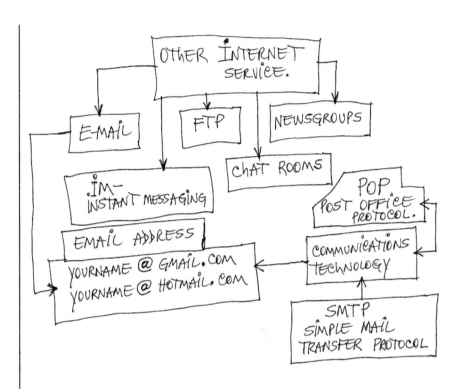

FORTYTHREE

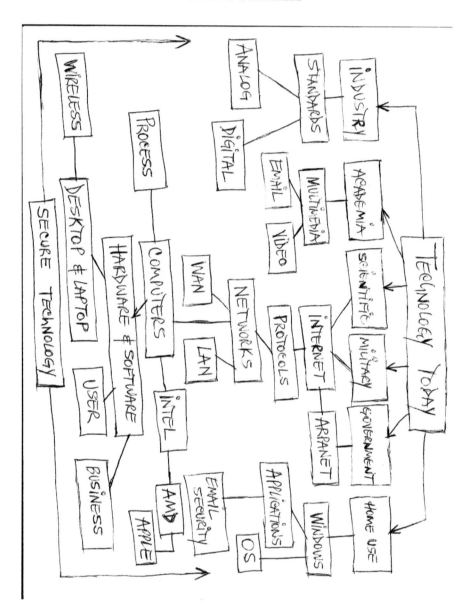

FORTYFOUR

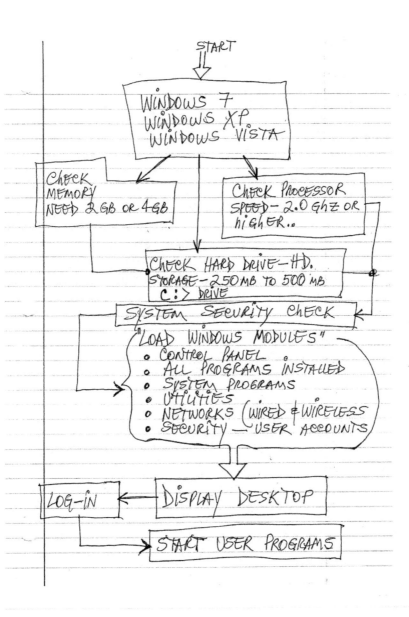

START

WINDOWS 7
WINDOWS XP.
WINDOWS VISTA

CHECK
MEMORY
NEED 2 GB OR 4 GB

CHECK PROCESSOR
SPEED — 2.0 GHz OR
hiGhER..

CHECK HARD DRIVE — HD.
STORAGE — 250 MB TO 500 MB
C:> DRIVE

SYSTEM SECURITY CHECK

"LOAD WINDOWS MODULES"
- CONTROL PANEL
- ALL PROGRAMS INSTALLED
- SYSTEM PROGRAMS
- UTILITIES
- NETWORKS (WIRED & WIRELESS)
- SECURITY — USER ACCOUNTS

LOG-IN

DISPLAY DESKTOP

START USER PROGRAMS

FORTYFIVE

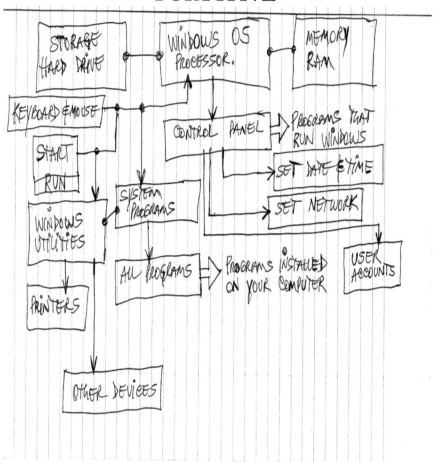

Attribution from: Patrick L. Lynch and Sarah Horton 2009
www.webstyleguide.com

• Graphic File Formats

The primary web file formats are gif (pronounced "jiff"), jpeg ("jay-peg"), and, to a much lesser extent, png ("ping") files. All three common web graphic formats are so-called bitmap graphics, made up of a checkerboard grid of thousands of tiny colored square picture elements, or pixels. Bitmap files are the familiar types of files produced by cell phone and digital cameras, and are easily created, edited, resized, and optimized for web use with such widely available tools as Adobe's Photoshop or Elements, Corel's Paint Shop Pro and Painter, and other photo editing programs.

For efficient delivery over the Internet, virtually all web graphics are compressed to keep file sizes as small as possible. Most web sites use both gif and jpeg images. Choosing between these file types is largely a matter of assessing:

- The nature of the image (is the image a "photographic" collection of smooth tonal transitions or a diagrammatic image with hard edges and lines?)
- The effect of various kinds of file compression on image quality
- The efficiency of a compression technique in producing the smallest file size that looks good
- **GIF Graphics**

The CompuServe Information Service popularized the Graphic Interchange Format (gif) in the 1980s as an efficient means to transmit images across data networks. In the early 1990s the original designers of the World Wide Web adopted gif for its efficiency and widespread familiarity. Many images on the web are in gif format, and virtually all web browsers that support graphics can display gif files. gif files incorporate a "lossless" compression scheme to keep file sizes at a minimum without compromising quality. However, gif files are 8-bit graphics and thus can only accommodate 256 colors.

- **GIF file compression**

The gif file format uses a relatively basic form of file compression (<u>Lempel Ziv Welch</u>, or lzw) that squeezes out inefficiencies in data storage <u>without losing data</u> or distorting the image. The lzw compression scheme is best at compressing images with large fields of homogeneous color, such as logos and diagrams. It is much less efficient at compressing complicated "photographic" pictures with many colors and complex textures (fig. 11.4).

Dithering

Full-color photographs can contain an almost infinite range of color values; gif images can contain no more than 256 colors. The process of reducing many colors to 256 or fewer is called <u>dithering</u>. With dithering, pixels of two colors are juxtaposed to create the illusion that a third color is present. Dithering a photographic image down to 256 colors produces an unpleasantly grainy image (fig. 11.5). In the past this technique was necessary to create images that would look acceptable on 256-color computer screens, but with today's full-color displays there is seldom any need to dither an image. If you need a wider range of colors than the gif format can handle, try using your image editor to save the image in both jpeg and png formats (described below), compare the resulting file sizes and image qualities, and pick the best balance of file size and image quality.

Improving GIF compression

You can take advantage of the characteristics of lzw compression to improve its efficiency and thereby reduce the size of your gif graphics. The strategy is to reduce the number of colors in your gif image to the minimum number necessary and to remove colors that are not required to represent the image. A gif graphic cannot have more than 256 colors, but it can have fewer. Images with fewer colors will compress more efficiently under lzw compression. For example, when creating gif graphics in Photoshop, don't save every file automatically with 256 colors. A simple gif image may look fine at 8, 16, or 32 colors, and the file size savings can be substantial. For maximum efficiency in gif graphics, use the minimum number of colors that gives you a good visual result.

Interlaced GIF

The conventional (noninterlaced) gif graphic downloads one line of pixels at a time from top to bottom, and browsers display each line of the image as it gradually builds on the screen. In interlaced gif files the image data is stored in a format that allows browsers that support this feature to build a low-resolution version of the full-sized gif picture on the screen while the file is downloading. Many people find the "fuzzy-to-sharp" animated effect of interlacing visually appealing, but the most important benefit of interlacing is that it gives the user a preview of the full picture while the picture downloads into the browser.

Interlacing is best for larger gif images such as illustrations of 200 × 100 pixels or greater. Interlacing is a poor choice for small gif graphics such as navigation bars, buttons, and icons. These small graphics will load onto the screen much faster if you keep them in conventional (noninterlaced) gif format. In general, interlacing has no significant effect on the file size of average gif graphics.

Transparent GIF

The gif format allows you to pick colors from the color lookup table of the gif to be transparent. You can use image-editing software such as Photoshop (and many shareware utility programs) to select colors in a gif graphic's color palette to become transparent. Usually the color selected for transparency is the background color in the graphic. Unfortunately, the transparent property is not selective; if you make a color transparent, every pixel in the graphic that shares that color will also become transparent, which can cause unexpected results.

Adding transparency to a gif graphic can produce disappointing results when the image contains anti-aliasing. If you use an image-editing program like Photoshop to create a shape set against a background color, Photoshop will smooth the shape by inserting pixels of intermediate colors along the shape's boundary edges. This smoothing, or anti-aliasing, improves the look of screen images by softening what would otherwise look like jagged edges. The trouble comes when you set the background color to transparent and then use the image on a Web page against a different background color. The anti-aliased pixels in the image will still correspond to the original background color. In the example below, when we change the background color from white to transparent (letting the gray web page background show through), an ugly white halo appears around the graphic (fig. 11.6).

The same problem exists with printing. Most browsers do not print background colors, and a transparent gif anti-aliased against a colored background will not blend smoothly into the white of the printed page.

JPEG graphics

The other graphic file format commonly used on the web to minimize graphics file sizes is the Joint Photographic Experts Group (jpeg) compression scheme. Unlike gif graphics, jpeg images are full-color images that dedicate at least 24 bits of memory to each pixel, resulting in images that can incorporate 16.8 million colors.

jpeg images are used extensively among photographers, artists, graphic designers, medical imaging specialists, art historians, and other groups for whom image quality and color fidelity is important. A form of jpeg file called "progressive jpeg" gives jpeg graphics the same gradually built display seen in interlaced gifs. Like interlaced gifs, progressive jpeg images often take longer to load onto the page than standard jpegs, but they do offer the user a quicker preview.

jpeg compression uses a sophisticated mathematical technique called a discrete cosine transformation to produce a sliding scale of graphics compression. You can choose the degree of compression you wish to apply to an image in jpeg format, but in doing so you also determine the image's quality. The more you squeeze a picture with jpeg compression, the more you degrade its quality. jpeg can achieve incredible compression ratios, squeezing graphics down to as much as one hundred times smaller than the original file. This is possible because the jpeg algorithm discards "unnecessary" data as it compresses the image, and it is thus called a "lossy" compression technique. Notice in figure 11.7 how increasing the jpeg compression progressively degrades the details of the image. The checkered pattern and the dark "noise" pixels in the compressed image are classic jpeg compression artifacts. Note the extensive compression noise and distortion present in the image below, particularly around the leading edge of the fish's head.

Save your original uncompressed images!

Once an image is compressed using jpeg compression, data is lost and you cannot recover it from that image file. Always save an uncompressed original file of your graphics or photographs as backup. If your digital camera produces jpeg images, set aside the "camera original" jpeg files and work with copies when you edit the files for web use. Each time you save or resave an image in jpeg format, the image is compressed further and the artifacts and noise in the image increase.

PNG graphics

Portable Network Graphic (png) is an image format developed by a consortium of graphic software developers as a nonproprietary alternative to the gif image format. As mentioned above, CompuServe developed the gif format, and gif uses the proprietary lzw compression scheme, which was patented by Unisys Corporation, meaning that any graphics tool developer making software that saved in gif format had to pay a royalty to Unisys and CompuServe. The patent has since expired, and software developers can use the gif format freely.

png graphics were designed specifically for use on web pages, and they offer a range of attractive features, including a full range of color depths, support for sophisticated image transparency, better interlacing, and automatic corrections for display monitor gamma. png images can also hold a short text description of the image's content, which allows Internet search engines to search for images based on these embedded text descriptions.

png supports full-color images and can be used for photographic images. However, because it uses lossless compression, the resulting file is much larger than with lossy jpeg compression. Like gif, png does best with line art, text, and logos—images that contain large areas of homogenous color with sharp transitions between colors. Images of this type saved in the png format look good and have a similar or even smaller file size than when saved as gifs. However, widespread adoption of the png format has been slow. This is due in part to inconsistent support in web browsers. In particular, Internet Explorer does not fully support all the features of png graphics. As a result, most images that would be suitable for png compression use the gif format instead, which has the benefit of full and consistent browser support. Photographs as JPEGs

jpeg image files are inherently full-color (24-bit) images, so preserving the correct colors in the files is not an issue. You should standardize on the jpeg format for any photographic or other full-color or grayscale image suitable for jpeg compression.

- **Diagrams and illustrations as vector graphics**

Most web page graphics are <u>bitmap (or "raster") images</u> composed of a grid of colored pixels. Complex diagrams or illustrations, however, should be created as <u>vector graphics</u> and then converted to raster formats like gif or <u>png</u> for the web. Vector graphics (also known as <u>PostScript</u> graphics) are composed of mathematical descriptions of lines and shapes. Although these graphics cannot be used directly to illustrate web pages without requiring users to have a special browser plug-in, there are three major reasons for producing complex diagrams in vector graphics programs:

- Illustrations are easier to draw and modify using vector-based illustration programs such as Adobe Illustrator;
- Vector graphics can be easily resized without loss of image quality; and
- Complex artwork created in such vector-based programs is a better investment of your illustration budget, because vector graphics also produce high-resolution images suitable for print.

Vector graphics can be viewed directly in the browser. Adobe's Flash format supports both vector and raster images. Several viewers support Scalable Vector Graphics, a file format developed by the World Wide Web Consortium. However, support for these formats is not native to older browsers, requiring users to install plug-ins to view the images. Your best bet is to create illustrations and diagrams using vector-based illustration software and then convert to gif or png for use on the web.

- **Archiving your web site graphics**

Always save a copy of your original graphics files, and make it a standard practice to create separate new files each time you make significant changes to an image, such as resizing it or changing the file format. After the close of a project all photos and artwork should be kept and stored at their full original resolution and in a format that does not compromise the image quality of the files through lossy image compression, as in jpeg. We prefer to archive every image generated in a project. Many small 8-bit gif or jpeg illustrations on the finished web page start out as much larger high-resolution files in Photoshop format. We save all the intermediate pieces, not just the original and final files. This will save you a lot of time later if you change your mind about the best file format for a graphic or need to modify it. If you have archived the full-color Photoshop or camera-original jpeg version of the graphic, you can easily create a new version in a different format. If you save only the final gifs, you will have lost your full-color version. If you save only the final jpegs, you will no longer have images without compression artifacts, and recompressing an image that already contains jpeg compression noise usually yields poor results.

Summary: Graphics file formats

All major browsers have native support for gif and jpeg graphics, as well as the basic features of png graphics. Browsers with the Adobe Flash plug-in support Flash vector graphics. In theory, you can use any of these graphic formats for the visual elements of your web pages. In practice, however, most web developers will continue to favor the gif format for most page design elements, diagrams, and images and will choose the jpeg format for photographs, complex "photographic" Advantages of GIF files

- gif is the most widely supported graphics format on the web
- gifs of diagrammatic images look better than jpegs
- gif supports transparency and interlacing

- ## <u>Advantages of JPEG images</u>

  - jpeg achieves huge compression ratios, which mean faster downloads
  - jpeg produces excellent results for most photographs and complex images
  - jpeg supports full-color (24-bit, true-color) images

  With permission;
  More info from: **www.webstyleguide.com**

Attribution from: Patrick L. Lynch and Sarah Horton 2009

Other Graphics Standards and Formats used today.__

- **Raster graphics**

Raster (or Bitmap) files store images as a group of pixels.

- ASE — Adobe Swatch
- ART — America Online proprietary format
- BLP — Blizzard Entertainment proprietary texture format
- BMP — Microsoft Windows Bitmap formatted image
- BTI — Nintendo proprietary texture format
- CD5 — Chasys Draw IES image
- CIT — Intergraph is a monochrome bitmap format
- CPT — Corel PHOTO-PAINT image
- CR2 — Canon camera raw format. Photos will have this format on some Canon cameras if the quality "RAW" is selected in camera settings.
- CUT — Dr. Halo image file
- DDS — DirectX texture file
- DIB — Device-Independent Bitmap graphic
- DjVu — DjVu for scanned documents
- EGT — EGT Universal Document, used in EGT SmartSense to compress PNG files to yet a smaller file
- Exif — Exchangeable image file format (Exif) is a specification for the image file format used by digital cameras
- GIF — CompuServe's Graphics Interchange Format
- GPL — GIMP Palette, using a textual representation of color names and RGB values
- GRF — Zebra Technologies proprietary format

- ICNS — file format use for **icons** in macOS. Contains bitmap images at multiple resolutions and bitdepths with alpha channel.
- ICO — a file format used for **icons** in Microsoft Windows. Contains small bitmap images at multiple resolutions and sizes.
- IFF (.iff, .ilbm, .lbm) — ILBM
- JNG — a single-frame MNG using JPEG compression and possibly an alpha channel.
- JPEG, JFIF (.jpg or .jpeg) — Joint Photographic Experts Group — a lossy image format widely used to display photographic images.
- JP2 — JPEG2000
- JPS — JPEG Stereo
- LBM — Deluxe Paint image file
- MAX — ScanSoft PaperPort document
- MIFF — ImageMagick's native file format
- MNG — Multiple Network Graphics, the animated version of PNG
- MSP — a file format used by old versions of Microsoft Paint. Replaced with BMP in Microsoft Windows 3.0
- NITF — A U.S. Government standard commonly used in Intelligence systems
- OTB - Over The Air bitmap, a specification designed by Nokia for black and white images for mobile phones
- PBM — Portable bitmap
- PC1 — Low resolution, compressed Degas picture file
- PC2 — Medium resolution, compressed Degas picture file
- PC3 — High resolution, compressed Degas picture file
- PCF — Pixel Coordination Format

- <u>PCX</u> — a lossless format used by ZSoft's PC Paint, popular at one time on <u>DOS</u> systems.

Vector graphics

Vector graphics use geometric primitives such as points, lines, curves, and polygons to represent images.

- **3DV** — 3-D wireframe graphics by Oscar Garcia
- **AMF** — Additive Manufacturing File Format
- **AWG** — Ability Draw
- **AI** — **Adobe Illustrator** Document
- **CGM** — Computer Graphics Metafile, an **ISO** Standard
- CDR — **CorelDRAW** Document
- CMX — **CorelDRAW** vector image
- **DXF** — ASCII Drawing Interchange file Format, used in **AutoCAD** and other CAD-programs
- E2D — 2-dimensional vector graphics used by the editor which is included in **JFire**
- EGT — EGT Universal Document, EGT Vector Draw images are used to draw vector to a website
- **EPS** — Encapsulated Postscript
- FS — FlexiPro file
- GBR — **Gerber file**
- ODG — **OpenDocument** Drawing
  - **MOVIE.BYU**
  - **RenderMan**
- **SVG** — Scalable Vector Graphics, employs **XML**
- **Scene description languages** (3D vector image formats)

- STL — Stereo Lithographic data format (see **STL (file format)**) used by various CAD systems and stereo lithographic printing machines. See above.
- **VRML** Uses .wrl extension — Virtual Reality Modeling Language, for the creation of 3D viewable web images.
- **X3D**
- SXD — **OpenOffice.org XML** (obsolete) Drawing
- V2D — voucher design used by the voucher management included in **JFire**
- VDOC — Vector file format used in AnyCut, CutStorm, DrawCut, DragonCut, FutureDRAW, MasterCut, SignMaster, VinylMaster software by **Future Corporation**
- VSD - Vector file format used by **Microsoft Visio**
- VSDX - Vector file format used by MS Visio and opened by **VSDX Annotator**
- VND — Vision numeric Drawing file used in **TypeEdit, Gravostyle**.
- **WMF** — Windows Meta File
- **EMF** — Enhanced (Windows) MetaFile, an extension to WMF
- ART — **Xara** — Drawing (superseded by XAR)
- XAR — **Xara** — Drawing

• **3D graphics**

3D graphics are 3D models that allow building models in real-time or non real-time 3D rendering.

- 3DMF — QuickDraw 3D Metafile (.3dmf)
- 3DM — OpenNURBS Initiative 3D Model (used by Rhinoceros 3D) (.3dm)
- 3MF — Microsoft 3D Manufacturing Format (.3mf)[2]
- 3DS — Legacy 3D Studio Model (.3ds)
- ABC — Alembic (computer graphics)
- AC — AC3D Model (.ac)
- AMF — Additive Manufacturing File Format
- AN8 — Anim8or Model (.an8)
- AOI — Art of Illusion Model (.aoi)
- ASM – PTC Creo assembly (.asm)
- B3D — Blitz3D Model (.b3d)
- BLEND — Blender (.blend)
- BLOCK — Blender encrypted blend files (.block)
- BMD3 — Nintendo GameCube first-party proprietary model format (.bmd)
- BDL (BMD4) — Nintendo Wii first-party proprietary model format 2006 - 2010 (.bdl)
- BRRES — Nintendo Wii first-party proprietary model format 2010+ (.brres)
- C4D — Cinema 4D (.c4d)
- Cal3D — Cal3D (.cal3d)
- CCP4 — X-ray crystallography voxels (electron density)
- CFL — Compressed File Library (.cfl)
- COB — Caligari Object (.cob)
- CORE3D — Coreona 3D Coreona 3D Virtual File(.core3d)
- CTM — OpenCTM (.ctm)
- DAE — COLLADA (.dae)
- DFF — RenderWare binary stream, commonly used by Grand Theft Auto III-era games as well as other RenderWare titles
- DPM — deepMesh (.dpm)

- DTS — Torque Game Engine (.dts)
- EGG — Panda3D Engine
- FACT — Electric Image (.fac)
- FBX — Autodesk FBX (.fbx)
- G — BRL-CAD geometry (.g)
- GLM — Ghoul Mesh (.glm)
- IOB - Imagine (3D modeling software) (.iob)
- JAS — Cheetah 3D file (.jas)
- LWO — Lightwave Object (.lwo)
- LWS — Lightwave Scene (.lws)
- LXO — Luxology Modo (software) file (.lxo)
- MA — Autodesk Maya ASCII File (.ma)
- MAX — Autodesk 3D Studio Max file (.max)
- MB — Autodesk Maya Binary File (.mb)
- MD2 — Quake 2 model format (.md2)
- MD3 — Quake 3 model format (.md3)
- MDX — Blizzard Entertainment's own model format (.mdx)
- MESH — New York University(.m)
- MESH — Meshwork Model (.mesh)
- MM3D — Misfit Model 3d (.mm3d)
- MPO — Multi-Picture Object — This JPEG standard is used for 3d images, as with the Nintendo 3DS
- MRC — voxels in cryo-electron microscopy
- NIF — Gamebryo NetImmerse File (.nif)
- OBJ — Wavefront .obj file (.obj)
- OFF — OFF Object file format (.off)
- OGEX — Open Game Engine Exchange (OpenGEX) format (.ogex)
- PLY — Polygon File Format / Stanford Triangle Format (.ply)
- PRC — Adobe PRC (embedded in PDF files)
- PRT – PTC Creo part (.prt)
- POV — POV-Ray document (.pov)
- R3D - Realsoft 3D (Real-3D) (.r3d)
- RWX — RenderWare Object (.rwx)
- SIA — Nevercenter Silo Object (.sia)
- SIB — Nevercenter Silo Object (.sib)
- SKP — Google Sketchup file (.skp)
- SLDASM — SolidWorks Assembly Document (.sldasm)

- SLDPRT — SolidWorks Part Document (.sldprt)
- SMD — Valve Studiomdl Data format. (.smd)
- U3D — Universal 3D file format (.u3d)
- VIM — Revizto visual information model format (.vimproj)
- VRML97 — VRML Virtual reality modeling language (.wrl)
- VUE — Vue scene file (.vue)
- VWX — Vectorworks (.vwx)
- WINGS — Wings3D (.wings)
- W3D — Westwood 3D Model (.w3d)
- X — DirectX 3D Model (.x)
- X3D — Extensible 3D (.x3d)
- Z3D — Zmodeler (.z3d)

- PDN — Paint.NET image file
- PGM — Portable graymap
- PI1 — Low resolution, uncompressed Degas picture file
- PI2 — Medium resolution, uncompressed Degas picture file. Also Portrait Innovations encrypted image format.
- PI3 — High resolution, uncompressed Degas picture file
- PICT, PCT — Apple Macintosh PICT image
- PNG — Portable Network Graphic (lossless, recommended for display and edition of graphic images)
- PNM — Portable anymap graphic bitmap image
- PNS — PNG Stereo
- PPM — Portable Pixmap (Pixel Map) image
- PSB — Adobe Photoshop Big image file (for large files)
- PSD, PDD — Adobe Photoshop Drawing

- PSP — Paint Shop Pro image
- PX — Pixel image editor image file
- PXM — Pixelmator image file
- PXR — Pixar Image Computer image file
- QFX — QuickLink Fax image
- RAW — General term for minimally processed image data (acquired by a digital camera)
- RLE — a run-length encoded image
- SCT — Scitex Continuous Tone image file
- SGI, RGB, INT, BW — Silicon Graphics Image
- TGA (.tga, .targa, .icb, .vda, .vst, .pix) — Truevision TGA (Targa) image
- TIFF (.tif or .tiff) — Tagged Image File Format (usually lossless, but many variants exist, including lossy ones)
- TIFF/EP (.tif or .tiff) — ISO 12234-2; tends to be used as a basis for other formats rather than in its own right.
- VTF — Valve Texture Format
- XBM — X Window System Bitmap
- XCF — GIMP image (from Gimp's origin at the eXperimental Computing Facility of the University of California)
- XPM — X Window System Pixmap

- **Page description language**
-

  - <u>DVI</u> — Device independent format
  - EGT — Universal Document can be used to store CSS type styles (*.egt)
  - <u>PLD</u>
  - <u>PCL</u>
  - <u>PDF</u> — Portable Document Format
  - <u>PostScript</u> (.ps, .ps.gz)
  - <u>SNP</u> — <u>Microsoft Access</u> Report Snapshot
  - <u>XPS</u>
  - <u>XSL-FO (Formatting Objects)</u>
  - Configurations, Metadata
    - <u>CSS</u> — Cascading Style Sheets
    - XSLT, XSL — <u>XML Style Sheet</u> (.xslt, .xsl)
    - TPL — <u>Web template</u> (.tpl)
    -

- **Personal information manager**

  - MSG — <u>Microsoft Outlook</u> task manager
  - ORG — <u>Lotus Organizer</u> PIM package
  - PST, OST — Microsoft Outlook email communication
  - SC2 — <u>Microsoft Schedule+</u> calendar

- **Presentation**

  - GSLIDES — <u>Google Drive</u> Presentation
  - KEY, KEYNOTE — <u>Apple Keynote</u> Presentation
  - NB — <u>Mathematica</u> Slideshow
  - NBP — Mathematica Player slideshow
  - ODP — <u>OpenDocument</u> Presentation

- OTP — OpenDocument Presentation template
- PEZ — Prezi Desktop Presentation
- POT — Microsoft PowerPoint template
- PPS — Microsoft PowerPoint Show
- PPT — Microsoft PowerPoint Presentation
- PPTX — Office Open XML Presentation
- PRZ — Lotus Freelance Graphics
- SDD — StarOffice's StarImpress
- SHF — ThinkFree Show
- SHOW — Haansoft(Hancom) Presentation software document
- SHW — Corel Presentations slide show creation
- SLP — Logix-4D Manager Show Control Project
- SSPSS — SongShow Plus Slide Show
- STI — OpenOffice.org XML (obsolete) Presentation template
- SXI — OpenOffice.org XML (obsolete) Presentation
- THMX — Microsoft PowerPoint theme template
- WATCH — Dataton Watchout Presentation

End of Common Graphic Formats.

Windows Graphics Pages

The Graphics presented in this book were created with No. 2 pencil and then Scanned in Hi Resolution and converted to .PDF

The format used is a new format I call **.gbf** Graphics Box Format, and may later become another Desktop Publishing Standard. All of the more common Standards used today are presented.

New Basic Computer Terms

Acceptable Use
Policy (AUP)
AUP: A set of rules and guidelines that are set up
to regulate Internet use and to protect the user
Active Cell
In a spreadsheet, the cell you are working
in. The cell is identified by a thick dark border.
Alignment
The way in which text lines up across a page. The text can be
right-aligned, centered, left-aligned, or fully-
aligned (justified).
Animated Clip
Art
A moving clip art graphic
Anti- Virus
An application or program designed to scan or search disks
or hard drives for viruses and repair files that it
finds
Application or
Software
Computer program -- Software that allows you to perfor
m a task or solve a specific problem. Programs that
allow you to accomplish certain tasks such as write letters
, analyze numbers, sort files, manage finances, draw
pictures, and play games.
Arrow Keys

The keys on the keyboard used to move the cursor up, down, left, or right.

Ascending

Order

One of two ways to sort a database. Numbers are arra nged from smallest to largest. Text is arranged in alphabetical order (A to Z) (See Descending)

Attachments

A file you add to an ema

il when you send it to someone else

Backup system A way of storing data in more than one location.

Baud Rate

The speed at which data signals are sent and receive d by a modem. The higher the baud rate the faster data is transferred

Bold

A style of text that makes a letter or word darker and thicker to stand out in a document.

Bomb

A type of virus designed to activate at a specific date and time on your computer

Browser

Software needed to be ab le to view information on the internet (See Internet Browser)

Button Bar or

Toolbar

A horizontal strip of buttons near the top of a window which provides shortcuts for common commands. Some programs allow the user to hide or display the bar, and customize the buttons.

Buttons

A hot spot used in multimedia ap

plications to navigate from one place to another or to activate elements such

as sound and animation.

Byte

A unit of storage usually made up of eight bits. It represents one character - a letter, digit, or symbol.

Cell

The intersection of each row and column in

a spreadsheet. Example:

Cell B5, Cell A202

Cell range

A continuous group of connected cells in a spreadsheet

Center align

Placement of test OR graphics in the center of a Word processing page or cell of a spreadsheet or table

Central

Processing Unit

(CPU)

Electronic circuits that interpret and execute instructions and communicates with the input, output, and storage devices.

Clip art

Drawings you can add to your documents, including cartoons, maps, symbols, and flags. Clip art comes with some programs or can be purchased separately.

Communication

Software

Provides the tools for connecting one computer with an other to enable sending an

d receiving information and

sharing files and resources.

Compact Disc

A disc on which a laser has digitally recorded information such as audio, video, or computer data.

Computer

An electronic device th
at operates under the control of a set of instructions that is stored in its memory unit. It
accepts data from an input device and
processes it into useful information, which it makes available on its
output device.

Copy

To make an exact dup
licate of information in your document, so yo
u can place the copy in
another lo
cation of
your document.

Copyright
Laws

Law that exist to protect those
who create a new idea or product

CPU (Central
Processing
Unit)

The brain of the computer or central processing unit. The main chip that allows computers to do millions of calculations per second and makes it possible for users to write letters and balance your checkbook.

Cursor

The flashing vertical line on the screen that
indicates where the next character will be typed.

Data

Raw unprocessed facts to be processed by the computer.

Database file

A collection of individual records in a database

Delete

To erase a letters, word paragraph or cell contents.
Use either the BACKSPACE key (erases to the left) or the
DELETE key (Erases to the right)

Delete key

A key used to erase characters to the right of the cursor.

Descending

Order

One of two ways to sort a database. Numbers are arranged
from largest to smallest. Text is arranged in reverse
alphabetical order (Z to A) (See Ascending Order)

Desktop

The background on the windows, menus, and dialog boxes
on a PC. It is designed to represent a desk.

Desktop

Publishing

Using features of word processing to
format and produce more sophisticated
documents with graphics and text,
such as flyer, brochures, or newsletters.

Edit

To make changes in a document or presentation and
therefore make it better.

e-mail

The ability to send and receive messages with a computer

Enter/Return The key used to begin a new line in a word
processo
r, or to enter information into a spreadsheet or database. It
is
the same as clicking OK in the dialog box.

Entry bar

Where the contents of the act
ive cell in a spreadsheet are displayed

Filter/query

A way to do a simple or complex search in a database to find record based on specific criteria.

Firewall

Technology that prevents users from inappropriate websites and protects the network from unauthorized users

Floppy Disk

A portable magnetic storage medium for computer data that allows users to randomly access information.

Font

The shape and style of text. Exampl
es: Verdana, Arial, and Times New Roman.

Format

To set margins, tabs, font, or line spacing in lay
out of a document. The way a do
cument or piece of a document
will look.

Formulas

A set of instructions or directions in a particular spreadsheet cell that tells the co
mputer exactly what mathematical
operations to do

Freeware

Software written and then donated to the public, so anyon
e is free to copy it and share it
with their friends. This i
s
not the same as shareware or commercial software
, because those are suppos
ed to be paid for.

Gif

(Graphic

Interchange
Format)
Pronounced "GIF". A simple file format for pictures an
d photographs that are compressed so they can be sent
quickly. Widely used on electronic bulletin boards and the
Internet, but cannot be used for high-end desktop
publishing. (See JPG)

Gigabyte
Approximately a billion bytes (or 1,000 megabytes).

Gigahertz
(GHZ)
A billion machine cycles per second.

Graphic
Images/pictures created, edited, and/or published using a
computer

Graphical
User
Interface
The use of graphical symbols instead of text commands to
control common computer functions such as copying
programs and disks.

Hacker
An unauthorized person who s
ecretly gains access to computer files

Hard Copy
A printed copy of computer output.

Hard disk
An internal disk, a metal platter coated with magnetic oxide
that can be magnetized to hold documents,
applications, or software. A fixed, large-capacity magnetic
storage medium for computer data.

Hardcopy

Output produced by a printer. Output from a computer that is "hard"... you can touch

Hardware

The physical components of the computer and any eq
uipment connected to it. Pieces
of the computer that you can
touch.

Highlight or
Select

To choose part of a document by clicking and dragging over it with the mouse to highlight the text; text must be selected to make changes in formatting.

Hoax

A computer virus that is in
tended to scare users into thinki
ng they really do have a virus

Home Page

An introductory screen on a web site, used to welc
ome visitors. A home page can in
clude special text or graphics
on which you click to jump to related information on other pages on the Web

Home Row

Keys on the keyboard from which all keystrokes are made. Fingers of the left hand are on ASDF and fingers on
the right hand are on JKL;

Host

Host computers are associated w
ith computer networks, online services, or bulletin board systems. They are
usually name given to a computer that directly connects the rest of a network to the Internet.

Hyperlink or
Hypertext

Special text when clicked jumps the user from their current location to another page or topic.
Icon
A small picture or symbol representing a computer hardware function or component.
Illustration
Clip art, graphics or drawings on a computer
Indent
To set the first line of a paragraph in from
the margin about 5 spaces. (USE THE TAB key!!!)
Ink-jet
Printer
A type of printer that forms letters on the page by shooting tiny electrically charged droplets of ink.
Input
To send data, text, documents to your computer's CPU. You can use ANY input device to do this
Input
Device
The hardware that is used to pass information into the co mputer. Any hardware device that lets you send data to your computer (i.e. keyboard, mouse, scanner)
Internet
A network of computers that provides information world-wide; also known as the information superhighway.
Internet
Browser
Provides access to the Internet
through a service provider by
using a graphical interface.
Jpeg
(Joint Photographic Experts

Group)
A standard for shrinking graphics so they can be sent faster between modems and take up less
space on your hard drive.
These graphics can be reduced to 5 percent of their original compressing
graphics to 30 or 40 percent of their original size results in minimal loss of quality

Keyboard
The hardware device used to enter letters into the computer (input device).

Keyword
A word or reference point to describe content
on a web page that search engines use to properly
index the page

Label
One of the three types of data you can put in a
spreadsheet cell. A label is
words or text that the
user need to read to understan
ding the meaning of the numbers.

Landscape
The page setup the permits a document to be printed in a horizontal position. (See portrait)

Laptop
A portable computer that can be taken with your where ever you to.

Laser Printer
A printer that uses both laser and photographic technology to produce high quality output.

Licenses Special agreements
in copyrighted programs that spell out what you can and cannot to with the

software you purchased, and how many computer(s) you
may put the software on.

Line spacing

The span between lines of text

(i.e.: Double Space, single space 1.5 spaces)

Linear

Moving in a straight line or path; a multimedia presentation
that moves in a straight line from

image to image (i.e. PowerPoint

presentations)

See NON-linear

Links

Connections that bridge one image, page, or word to another
by clicking on a highlighted word or

phrase

Mainframes

Classified by size, the second largest classi

fication of computers. Much larger than desktops or

laptop computers

Megabyte (Mb)

Approximately a million bytes.

Megahertz (MHz)

One million machine cycles per second.

Memory

Primary storage that works with the CPU to hold
instructions and data in order to be processed.

Microcomputers

Personal computers or desktop computers.

Modem

The device that allows your computer to talk to other
computers over a telephone line.

Monitor

An output device with a screen used to show computer images. A video or computer display device.

Mouse
A tool used to move the cursor and pointer on the screen (input device).

Multimedia
To use a combination of text, pictures, sounds, movies, and/or animation.

Network
A system of connected comp uters that allows a sharing of fi les and equipment. There are two types of networks: local area network (LAN) and wide area network (WAN)

Non-linear
Not moving in a straight line or path; a multimedia presentation that transitions from one image to another in an order that is preset, but not necessarily in a straight path. - Example: a non-linear presentation can transition from image 1 to image 3 and back to image 1 using menus and branching to move around the pages

Notebook
A personal computer that can fit into a briefcase.

Numeric Keypad
The portion of the keyboard, usually on the right hand side of a full keyboard, used to enter numbers and basic math functions (+ - * /) quickly.

Online Resources
Internet informati on available to a computer user

Online Safety

Precautions taken to protect personal information and images from being misused by others.

Operating systems software (OS)

The set of programs that must be on your computer for the computer to boot properly. It controls all the overall activity of a computer and the way other program and your desktop work.

Output

Central processing unit executes computer instructions. Memory holds data and programs temporarily.

Output Device

The hardware that receives and di splays information comi ng from the computer.

Page Setup

The term in reference to the way a document is formatted to print

Password

A code for the security protection to allow access to a computer or programs.

Paste

To insert the last information to be cut or copied into a document; can be used to move information in or between documents

PDA (Personal digital assistant)

Classified by size, the smallest classification of computers. It is a handheld computer. Usually performing on one or two specific functions.

Portrait
The default page setup that prints the document vertically.
(See landscape)
Presentation Graphics
Provides the tools
for creating graphics that represent data
in a visual, easily understood format.
Print
To create a paper copy (or hard copy)
of the information on the computer screen.
Printer
A hardware device used to make a copy on paper (output
device).
Processing
Output devices make processed data available to the user.
Public Domain
Software written and then donated to the public. Anyone can
use and copy public domain software
free of charge, but it is not always the same quality as
commercial software
RAM
Random access memory. Memory that the co
mputer user can access. It can be changed if
necessary (resaving a word pr
ocessing document). The computer's working memory
ROM (Read only memory)
Read ONLY Memory. Memory that c
ontains programs and data th
at are permanently recorded
when the computer is built. Information stays in memory
even when the computer shuts down.
Save
To store information on a floppy disk, hard drive or CD for
later use. Work should be saved often,

every 5 or 10 minutes, to make sure th
e latest changes are safely recorded
Save As
To save a document with a new name or to a new location
on your hard drive
Search
To look for specific inform
ation on the internet or computer
Search Engines
Software that searches, gathers, and identifies information
from a database based on an index,
keywords or titles.
Search Strategies
There are 3 basic ways to begin a search
: 1. Try to guess the URL; 2. Use Subject directories
provided by some search engines; 3. Use a S
earch engine for large searches using unique
keywords or combinations of keywords to narrow a search
Security
Protection of a computer, its files, or a computer network
from use without permission of the
owner or owners
Server
A special computer used to store programs and
files, and then sends it out to other computers one
or all at a time
Shareware
A form of free software; however, the au
thor of shareware hopes
you will make a voluntary
contribution for using the product. Software that can be tried
before you purchase

Softcopy
Monitor output. (See hard copy)
Software
A program that consists of instructions used to control hardware and accomplish tasks. The
programs or instructions that
tell the computer what to do.
Spreadsheets
Provides the tools fo
r working with numbers and allows
you to create and edit electronic
spreadsheets in managing and analyzing information.
Stand Alone Computer
A computer that does not rely upon any other computer or server to work; it is not networked and
does not share resources.
Storyboard
A graphic organizer used for planning and developing a multimedia presentation. The contents,
layout, and formatting of each card/slide and th
e linking together of the cards/slides is
storyboarding.
Supercomputers
Classified by size, th
e largest classification of computers.
Telecommunication
The act of sending an
d receiving information,
such as data, text, pictures, voice, and video
electronically. The exchange of information can be within a building or around the globe.
Text
Words on a page, in a spreadsheet or database
Thesaurus

A feature in most word processors used to
replace a word in a document with one that is more
suitable and adds variety to your writing
URL Address
Website address (Example:
http://www.cms.k12.nc.us
)
User Name
First part of an e-mail address.
Vandalism
The intentional act of destroying computer files or computer
networks.
Virus
A computer program designed to damage computer files
Web address
Universal Resource Locator
(URL) Example: www.cms.k12.nc.us
Word Processing
Using keyboarding skills to produce documen
ts such as letters, reports, manuals, and newsletters;
used for documents that are
largely text-based (words)
Word Processor
Provides the tools for entering and revising text, adding
graphical elements, formatting and
printing documents.
Word Wrap
When text automatically flows from one line to the
beginning of the next line without the user
having to press the Enter/Return key. The co
mputer decides where the best place to begin the
next new line is.

Workspace
The typing area
on your computer screen
Worm
A computer file designed to do damage that goes through a
computer and possibly a network
WWW
(world wide web)
One small part of the Internet that allows acc
ess to text, graphics, sound, and video. Free
information can be found on the world wide web.
WYSIWYG
[Pronounced: "Wissy wig")
WYSIWYG is an acronym for "What You See Is Wh
at You Get" and is pronounced "wizzy wig."
WYSIWYG simply means that the text and graphics shown
on your screen exactly match your printouts.

End of New Basic Computer Terms.

This is not the end.

www.ingramcontent.com/pod-product-compliance
Lightning Source LLC
LaVergne TN
LVHW052309060326
832902LV00021B/3772